Step 1
Go to www.openlightbox.com

Step 2
Enter this unique code

ZJGYVK9PX

Step 3
Explore your interactive eBook!

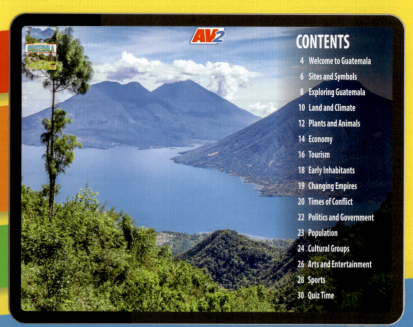

AV2 is optimized for use on any device

Your interactive eBook comes with...

Contents
Browse a live contents page to easily navigate through resources

Audio
Listen to sections of the book read aloud

Videos
Watch informative video clips

Weblinks
Gain additional information for research

Slideshows
View images and captions

Try This!
Complete activities and hands-on experiments

Key Words
Study vocabulary, and complete a matching word activity

Quizzes
Test your knowledge

Share
Share titles within your Learning Management System (LMS) or Library Circulation System

Citation
Create bibliographical references following APA, CMOS, and MLA styles

This title is part of our AV2 digital subscription

1-Year Grades K–5 Subscription
ISBN 978-1-7911-3320-7

Access hundreds of AV2 titles with our digital subscription.
Sign up for a FREE trial at www.openlightbox.com/trial

The digital components of this book are guaranteed to stay active for at least five years from the date of publication.

CENTRAL AMERICA
GUATEMALA

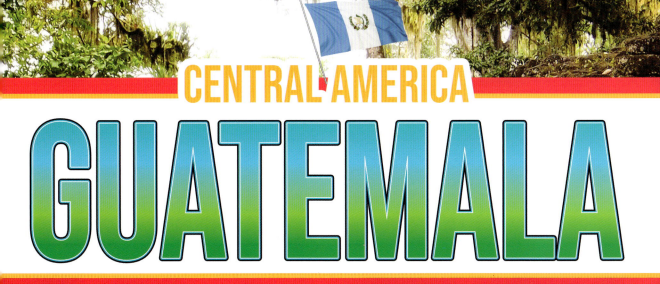

CONTENTS

Interactive eBook Code 2
Welcome to Guatemala 4
Sites and Symbols 6
Exploring Guatemala 8
Land and Climate 10
Plants and Animals 12
Economy 14
Tourism 16
Early Inhabitants 18
Changing Empires 19
Times of Conflict 20
Politics and Government 22
Population 23
Cultural Groups 24
Arts and Entertainment 26
Sports 28
Quiz Time 30
Key Words/Index 31

WELCOME TO GUATEMALA

From the ruins of its ancient temples and pyramids to the diversity of its many peoples, Guatemala is one of Central America's most vibrant countries. Guatemala's natural landscapes, citizens, and culture have all faced highs and lows throughout the country's long history. At one time, Guatemala was the center of the mighty **Mayan civilization**. More recently, it has had to rebuild after a brutal **civil war**. Today, the people and government of Guatemala are working to heal the wounds of their past and strengthen their future.

Eye on Guatemala

Capital
Guatemala City

Population
18.3 million (2024 estimate)

Official Language
Spanish

National Coat of Arms

National Flag

National Anthem
"*Himno Nacional de Guatemala*"
("National Anthem of Guatemala")

Currency
Quetzal

SITES AND SYMBOLS

Guatemala has its own unique identity. It uses a variety of symbols to represent this identity to the world. These symbols showcase the people, history, culture, and natural beauty of the country.

What's in a Name?

The Republic of Guatemala is the official name for Guatemala today. The exact origin of the *Guatemala* part of the name is not known. Some think it came from the Indigenous word *quauhtemallan*, or "land of trees." This term might have been used to describe the thick rainforests that once blanketed the land. Others believe the name is derived from the Indigenous word *guhatezmalha*, or "mountain that vomits water." This may refer to the massive volcano that towers above Antigua Guatemala, one of the country's former capital cities.

Palacio Nacional de la Cultura Completed in 1943, the National Palace was once the center of Guatemala's government. Today, it is a museum and symbol of the country's history, culture, and people. Important government ceremonies continue to be held here to this day.

National Tree
The ceiba has been Guatemala's national tree since 1955. It was chosen because it is a sacred symbol for the Maya. They consider it to be the "tree of life."

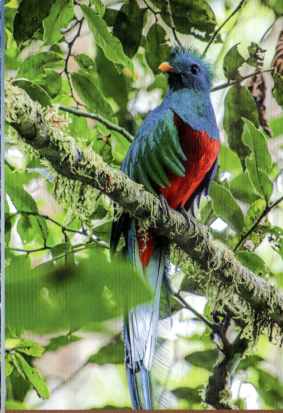

National Bird
The resplendent quetzal was named Guatemala's national bird in 1871. It was chosen because of its importance to the Maya, who saw it as a symbol of freedom and light.

National Instrument
The marimba was an important symbol in Guatemala even before it was named the national instrument in 1978. This instrument has long played a major role in Guatemalan music and celebrations.

National Flower
La Monja Blanca, one of the more than 500 species of orchid found in Guatemala, has been the national flower since 1934. To Guatemalans, it represents art, beauty, and peace.

EXPLORING GUATEMALA

Covering an area of 42,042 square miles (108,888 square kilometers), Guatemala is Central America's third-largest country, after Nicaragua and Honduras. Guatemala shares its borders with several other countries. To the north and west, it is bordered by Mexico. To the northeast, Guatemala reaches Belize, and to the southeast, Honduras. Directly south of Guatemala is the country of El Salvador. Guatemala borders two major bodies of water. The Pacific Ocean sits to the southwest, while the Caribbean Sea is to the east.

❶ Guatemala City
Founded in 1776, Guatemala City is both Guatemala's capital and its largest city. The city is the center of government and industry. It is also the country's cultural center, with museums, art galleries, and stunning **architecture**. Theater, dance, and musical performances draw visitors to the capital.

❷ The Volcano of Fire
Guatemala is home to more than 30 volcanoes. One of its most **active** is the Volcán de Fuego. The Maya named it *Chi'gag*, which means "where the fire is." This volcano sometimes erupts every 15 minutes. Most eruptions are small. The last major eruption took place in 2018.

❸ Lake Atitlán
Lake Atitlán, which plunges to a depth of 1,116 feet (340 meters), is the deepest lake in Central America. It is also a caldera lake, meaning it formed from volcanic activity. Today, Lake Atitlán sits among a combination of mountains, volcanoes, and fields of wildflowers.

❹ Candelaria Caves
These limestone caves are located in the north-central part of Guatemala. They are known for their stunning rock formations and underground rivers. Scientists have found **artifacts** in chambers within these caves that indicate the Maya used them for ceremonies and rituals.

LAND AND CLIMATE

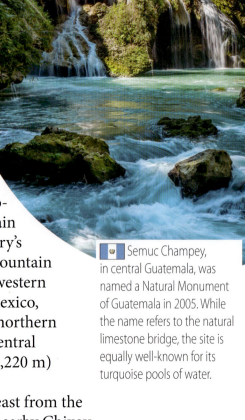

Guatemala is made up of three main geographic regions. The coastal regions are lowland areas located along the Pacific and Caribbean coasts. In the northeast is a lowland region known as El Petén. Its rugged terrain includes low hills, caves, and dense, swampy jungles.

Guatemala's mountainous region covers about two-thirds of the land. The nation has three major mountain chains. The Sierra del Lacandón is found in the country's northwest. Central America's highest non-volcanic mountain range, the Sierra de Los Cuchumatanes, is located in western Guatemala. The Sierra Madre de Chiapas begins in Mexico, runs through Guatemala and Honduras, and ends in northern El Salvador. Volcán Tajumulco is the tallest peak in Central America. This **dormant** volcano towers 13,845 feet (4,220 m) above western Guatemala.

The Motagua is Guatemala's longest river. It runs east from the mountains and empties into the Caribbean Sea. The nearby Chixoy River flows in a different direction. It winds east, then north, and then finally northwest through Mexico to the Bay of Campeche.

Semuc Champey, in central Guatemala, was named a Natural Monument of Guatemala in 2005. While the name refers to the natural limestone bridge, the site is equally well-known for its turquoise pools of water.

Located in the jungle near the Caribbean coast, the Seven Altars are considered one of Guatemala's most beautiful natural wonders. They consist of seven waterfalls and pools that flow over a terraced rock formation.

Guatemala is known as one of the most thunderstorm-prone areas in North America.

Guatemala's climate varies from region to region. The higher, mountainous areas have average temperatures of 61° Fahrenheit (16° Celsius). Temperatures in central Guatemala range from 50° to 85°F (10° to 29°C). Guatemala's coastal temperatures average 90°F (32°C) or more during the day and 70°F (21°C) at night. From July to October, Guatemala has a **tropical storm** season. Hurricanes and cyclones frequently blow in off the coasts at this time of year.

Seasonal Guatemala

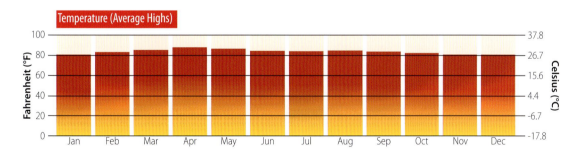

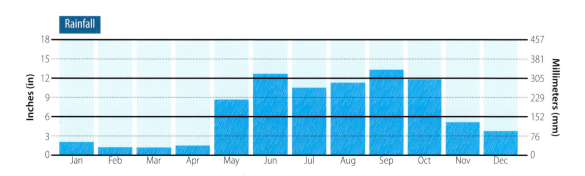

GUATEMALA 11

PLANTS AND ANIMALS

Guatemala's different landscapes and climates support a variety of **ecosystems**. These unique environments are home to diverse plant and animal species. However, many plants and animals that were once common in Guatemala are now **endangered**. Efforts are being made to protect them in nature preserves such as the Maya Biosphere Reserve, in the country's north.

Epiphytes include a variety of plants, ranging from mosses to orchids. A tree can have more than one type of epiphyte growing on it.

With its abundance of forested areas, Guatemala has many different types of trees. Palm, mahogany, sapodilla, and ceiba trees grow in the rainforests. Mangrove forests are found in wetland and coastal areas. Oak and pine forests are found in the mountains.

Cloud forests surround some of Guatemala's tallest and most barren peaks. Plants must adapt to this rocky, low-soil terrain. Several types of epiphytes, or "air plants," can be found in cloud forests. These rootless plants grow on trees and absorb the water they need from mist in the air.

More than 250 species of mammals are found in Guatemala. Mountain lions and jaguars are the largest of the country's wild cat species. Another wild cat, the jaguarundi, is known for its varying fur colors. These cats have gray fur in forested areas and red fur in drier, more barren places. Other mammals living in Guatemala include deer, monkeys, and tapirs.

While Central American spider monkeys can be found in Guatemala's forests, their population is decreasing and they are in danger of disappearing.

🇬🇹 The king vulture lives mainly in or near Guatemala's lower-elevation forests. It typically chooses areas that have been undisturbed by humans.

Approximately 750 bird species make their home in Guatemala. Some are **endemic** to specific parts of the country. The bearded screech owl and horned guan, for instance, are found only in western Guatemala and the country's central highlands. Other birds are more widespread. Toucans, parrots, and wild turkeys reside mainly in forested areas. Herons and storks frequent the country's coastal and wetland areas.

Coastal areas also host a variety of sea creatures. Manatees swim the waters along the Caribbean coast. Sea turtles come ashore to bury their eggs in protected areas. Morelet's crocodiles have wide snouts that make them look like alligators. They are known to lurk beneath the surface of the water waiting to surprise their **prey**.

🇬🇹 Morelet's crocodiles tend to hunt for food at dusk or later, spending much of their day basking in the sunlight. Prey animals include birds, lizards, and large fish.

Guatemala Bits

Approximately **1,000 species** of orchids can be found in Guatemala.

The Maya Biosphere Reserve is the **largest** single rainforest in Central America. It covers **20 percent** of Guatemala's total area.

A total of **18 venomous snake** species can be found in Guatemala.

ECONOMY

In spite of the challenges it has faced, Guatemala has the strongest economy in Central America, growing at about 4 percent per year. In 2024, the country had a **gross domestic product (GDP)** of more than $100 billion. The government is working to improve education, create more jobs, and protect the country's natural resources and environment.

Guatemala has long been an agricultural nation, and that industry continues to make money today. In 2024, agriculture contributed about $7 billion to the country's GDP. Approximately 27 percent of working Guatemalans have jobs in agriculture. Some of Guatemala's main crops are coffee, sugar, bananas, and a spice called cardamom.

Manufacturing accounts for close to one-quarter of Guatemala's GDP. Top **exports** include textiles, clothes, and processed foods. Large factories located near Guatemala City produce medicine, chemicals, and plastics. Approximately 15 percent of Guatemala's workforce is employed in manufacturing.

Guatemala exports more than $12 million worth of berries each year. The most lucrative crop is the blackberry, but blueberries, strawberries, and raspberries are also grown.

The K'iche' of Guatemala's midwestern highlands are known for the production of hand-crafted palm leaf hats. The traditions of hat-making have been passed down through generations.

Puerto Quetzal is Guatemala's largest port on the Pacific coast. More than 5.5 million tons (5 million metric tons) of cargo transit through it every year.

The largest and fastest-growing sector in the country is the service industry. Tourism, hospitality, finance, and telecommunications contribute significantly to Guatemala's economy. More than half of working Guatemalans have jobs in this sector.

Guatemala relies on **imports** from other countries. Major products brought into the country include fertilizer, machinery, transport equipment, fuel, and grain. Guatemala's main trading partner is the United States. However, since 1991, Guatemala has been part of the Central American Common Market. This group promotes trade between its five member countries—Guatemala, Honduras, Nicaragua, El Salvador, and Costa Rica.

Even with its growing economy, Guatemala still struggles with poverty and unemployment. Many Guatemalans move to other countries, such as the United States, to find jobs. The $15 billion they send home each year contributes more to Guatemala's economy than its major exports.

Guatemala GDP by Sector

Guatemala has a GDP of about $104.4 billion. Services, industry, and agriculture are the biggest contributors.

Services 61.3%
Industry 22.3%
Agriculture 9.8%
Other 6.6%

TOURISM

🇬🇹 Hiking to volcano summits is a popular activity in Guatemala. A hike to the top of the Atitlán volcano offers stunning views of the San Pedro volcano and Lake Atitlán.

Sandy beaches, ancient ruins, and a range of natural wonders draw millions of visitors to Guatemala each year. In 2024, the country welcomed more than 3 million tourists. This was an increase of 15 percent from the previous year.

Many who come to Guatemala seek adventure and experiences with nature. Surfers can find rideable waves along both of the country's coasts. Whitewater rafters brave rivers such as the Rio Dulce. Hikers climb to the cloud forests of the Sierra Madre. **Spelunkers** can explore a world of underground wonders in the northern region of El Petén.

The rainforests of the Maya Biosphere Reserve shelter many protected species. Tikal National Park is also located in the reserve. Tikal is the site of an ancient Mayan city. More than 200,000 people come to Tikal every year to see the remains of the city's homes, gathering places, sacred pyramids, and temples. Many other ancient cities are also open for tourists to explore. Uaxactun, Tayasal, and El Mirador are some of Guatemala's other ancient cities.

🇬🇹 At one time the largest city in the Americas, El Mirador is now found deep in the jungle near the Mexican border. Only about 2,000 to 3,000 people visit per year, due to its remote location.

Guatemala Bits

- Tikal is home to one of the **tallest Mayan pyramids** in the world. Pyramid IV is **213 feet** (65 m) tall.
- The number of tourists visiting Guatemala is expected to grow to **4 million** by **2028**.
- The **Chichicastenango market** has been in operation for more than **500 years**.

Tourists also enjoy exploring the modern cities and villages of Guatemala. Guatemala City has many impressive buildings that were inspired by Spanish architecture. The National Palace, National Library, National Archaeological Museum, and La Merced, a historic cathedral that serves as the center for Guatemala's Holy Week celebrations, are all found in the city. The Tower of the Reformer, also known as the Eiffel Tower of Guatemala, is visited by many tourists. The monument was built in honor of President General Justo Rufino Barrios.

Markets are a common sight throughout Guatemala. They are a gathering place for vendors, friends, and family. The market in Chichicastenango is the largest in Guatemala and attracts many international visitors. Located in the central park of the town, its vendors pack their stalls with brightly colored fruit, vegetables, spices, textiles, clothing, and crafts.

The *Museo del Café*, or Museum of Coffee, is located on a coffee plantation just outside Antigua. It provides an overview of how coffee is made, from bean to brew.

A variety of products, ranging from fruit and vegetables to artisan textiles and musical instruments, are sold at the Chichicastenango market.

EARLY INHABITANTS

People have lived in Guatemala for at least 14,000 years. It is believed that the first people arrived from the north. These early inhabitants were **nomadic**. They were skilled hunters and fishers who likely arrived in the area in pursuit of their prey animals.

By about 2500 BC, the Olmec people came to Guatemala from Mexico. They introduced advances in farming to the people living there. Permanent settlements began to form, and the residents grew crops such as corn, beans, and squash to feed their growing populations.

Beginning in about 1800 BC, the Maya rose to power. They had a very sophisticated and advanced society. At its height, the Mayan civilization controlled southern Mexico and much of Central America. Guatemalan cities, such as El Mirador and Tikal, became important centers for culture and trade.

By 900 AD, the Mayan civilization came to an end. No one is sure what caused its decline, but over the next 600 years, the once united civilization broke into separate groups. In Guatemala, the K'iche' and Kaqchikel rose to power. The K'iche' controlled much of the territory in Guatemala when the Spanish arrived in the 16th century AD.

Archaeological studies in the ruins of Tak'alik Ab'aj have uncovered a large number of Olmec and Mayan jade sculptures and masks, indicating that the city successfully transitioned from one civilization to the next.

A series of Mayan murals in the ancient ruins of San Bartolo have provided researchers with insight into Mayan mythology and beliefs. The murals are believed to tell the origins of the Maya and their history.

CHANGING EMPIRES

In 1524, a group of Spanish **conquistadors** led by Pedro de Alvarado arrived in Guatemala. An army of more than 30,000 K'iche' fought to defend their land but were defeated by the Spanish and their advanced weapons. Thousands more K'iche' were killed by diseases brought by the Spanish, such as smallpox, influenza, and measles.

After the battle, Guatemala became a province of New Spain. Control of the area fell to a small group of Spanish landowners. These men gained immense wealth and power growing crops such as cotton, sugar, and coffee.

The Spanish enforced a system called **encomienda**. It gave Spanish landowners the right to **enslave** Native Americans and force them to both speak Spanish and practice the Roman Catholic religion. Slaves brought from Africa also became part of this system. Anyone who refused to accept encomienda was put to death. Slavery was not abolished in Guatemala until 1824.

After 300 years of Spanish rule, Guatemala declared its independence in 1821. Two years later, Guatemala joined the United Provinces of Central America, a **federation** consisting of Guatemala, Costa Rica, Honduras, Nicaragua, and El Salvador. The union did not last long, and Guatemala became an independent nation in 1839.

Pedro de Alvarado became Guatemala's first governor in 1527. He served in this position until his death in 1541.

TIMES OF CONFLICT

From the mid-19th century to the mid-20th century, Guatemala experienced political instability and the rise of military **dictators** who used force and violence to maintain power. The first was José Rafael Carrera, who ruled between 1844 and 1865. Indigenous communities, particularly the Maya, had limited rights and faced discrimination and other mistreatment throughout this period.

In 1944, Guatemala held its first fair election. Juan José Arévalo became president. Guatemala entered into a period known as "Ten Years of Spring," because of the positive changes Arévalo made to the government and public services. Jacobo Árbenz Guzmán was elected president in 1951. He announced plans to redistribute land away from the country's major landowners and give it to a greater number of Guatemalans.

Before becoming president, José Rafael Carrera was a soldier. He led a peasant army that conquered Guatemala City and brought down the existing government.

GUATEMALA TIMELINE

14,000 years ago

FIRST PEOPLES
Nomadic peoples arrive in Guatemala, traveling there from the north.

2500 BC

BUILDING SETTLEMENTS
The Olmec come from Mexico and begin to build settlements throughout Guatemala.

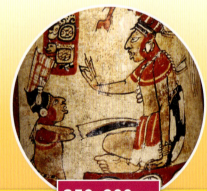

250–900 AD

MAYAN INFLUENCE
Guatemala comes under Mayan control. The Maya bring advances in politics and culture to the area.

20 CENTRAL AMERICA

Landowners felt threatened by these plans, as did many others who did not want to see the **status quo** upset. In 1954, the military, supported by Guzmán's opponents, staged a **coup** that removed him from power. In the years that followed, Guatemala was ruled by a series of dictators once more. The country entered into another long period of political instability and violence.

The 1980s saw the Guatemalan army hunt down rebel forces in rural areas. Attacks on Indigenous villages became common.

In the 1960s, civil war broke out between the government and various rebel groups. This conflict lasted for 36 years and resulted in the deaths of hundreds of thousands of people, the majority of whom were Maya. When the war ended in 1996, Guatemala enacted a peace agreement that aimed to address the issues that had caused the conflict. These included poverty, inequality, and discrimination.

Since the signing of the agreement, Guatemala has worked to honor its mandate. **Corruption**, poverty, and gang violence are still high. However, in recent years, the country has begun to make progress in strengthening its democracy and addressing its human rights issues.

1524–1821

SPANISH CONTROL
The Spanish rule Guatemala for almost 300 years, until its independence in 1821.

1996

END OF THE WAR
After 36 years of brutality, Guatemala's civil war comes to an end.

2024

A NEW PRESIDENT
Bernardo Arévalo, the son of Juan José Arévalo, becomes president of Guatemala.

POLITICS AND GOVERNMENT

Guatemala is a **democratic republic**. Its government is made up of three separate branches. The president leads the executive branch and also acts as the country's head of state. The president is supported by a vice president and the Council of Ministers. Council members are chosen by the president. Each member oversees a specific government department, such as education, defense, or healthcare.

Guatemala's legislative branch is made up of a 158-member **congress**. Its main responsibility is the passing of new laws. However, its members also monitor the work of the president and other areas of government.

The judicial branch ensures that the country's laws are being upheld. The highest court in the judicial branch is the Supreme Court. It is made up of 13 judges who are elected by Congress.

Karin Herrera became Guatemala's 18th vice president in 2024. Prior to her political career, she was a biologist and teacher.

Guatemala's Congress is unicameral, meaning that it consists of one group of lawmakers. They create and vote on laws as a whole.

POPULATION

Nearly 18 million people call Guatemala home. Almost half of Guatemalans live in **rural** areas. After Guatemala City, Villa Nueva is the country's largest city, with a population of more than 600,000. Other large cities in Guatemala include Mixco, Petapa, and Quetzaltenango.

While Guatemala's economy has grown, there is still a large gap between the wealthy and the poor. More than 50 percent of Guatemalans earn $2 or less per day. Jobs are often hard to find or do not pay well. Many schools are not funded or maintained. Nearly 30 percent of Guatemalans over the age of 15 cannot read or write.

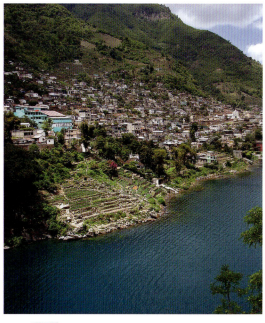
San Antonio Palopó is a rural village on the shores of Lake Atitlán. Its population is about 3,600.

Guatemala has one of the youngest populations in Central America. More than 30 percent of its people are under 14 years old. Due to improvements to its healthcare system, Guatemala also has one of the fastest-growing populations in Central America. Each year, Guatemala's population increases by about 1.5 percent.

Guatemalan children aged 7 to 14 are required to attend school, with the government providing free education. Even so, only about 80 percent of children complete their primary education and less than 30 percent continue to high school.

CULTURAL GROUPS

Guatemala has the largest Indigenous population in Central America. About 40 percent of the people living in Guatemala are Maya, and the country is home to more than 20 Mayan groups. The K'iche' is the largest, with a population of more than 1 million people. Many descendants of the Maya live in and around the city of Quetzaltenango.

Other Indigenous groups in Guatemala include the Garifuna and Xinca. Most Garifuna are of African and Mayan background. They are descended from slaves brought to Guatemala in the late 1800s. A small number of Xinca live in the remote areas of southeastern Guatemala. It is believed that their ancestors were living in Guatemala since before the Maya arrived.

More than half of Guatemala's population is Ladino. Ladinos have Spanish and Indigenous ancestors. Ladino culture has had a large influence on the traditional dishes, music, arts, and dance of Guatemala. A small percentage of Guatemalans have solely European lineage, mostly Spanish. Spanish culture has deeply influenced the language, beliefs, architecture, and traditions in Guatemala.

The Garifuna have been successful at maintaining their culture, with elders passing their knowledge on to younger generations. Local and national celebrations often feature Garifuna music and dances.

Roman Catholicism was once the main religion in Guatemala. Today, 45 percent of the population is Catholic. Just over 40 percent are Protestant, which is another form of Christianity. Small populations of people practice Judaism, Buddhism, and Islam. Many people of Maya and other Indigenous descent continue to practice their own systems of belief. Some practice religious traditions that combine Mayan beliefs with those of Roman Catholicism.

Spanish is Guatemala's official language. Approximately 70 percent of Guatemalans speak it as their native language. Nearly 30 percent of Guatemalans speak traditional Mayan languages. Throughout different periods in Guatemala's history, Indigenous people were punished for speaking their languages. Today, the various groups work to ensure their languages survive and are able to be passed from one generation to the next.

All Saints Day observances in Guatemala combine Indigenous and Catholic traditions. Known as a day to honor the dead, Guatemala's Catholic community creates giant kites in their honor. It is hoped that the kites will guide the spirits back to their loved ones.

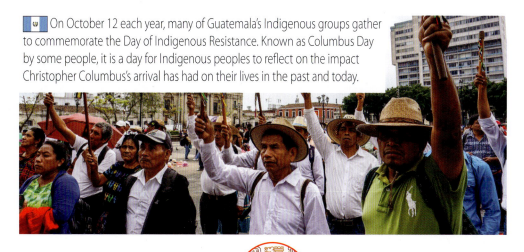

On October 12 each year, many of Guatemala's Indigenous groups gather to commemorate the Day of Indigenous Resistance. Known as Columbus Day by some people, it is a day for Indigenous peoples to reflect on the impact Christopher Columbus's arrival has had on their lives in the past and today.

Guatemala Bits

The Xinca make up **less than 2 percent** of Guatemala's population.

There are a total of **25 languages** spoken in Guatemala. These include **22 Mayan languages**.

Approximately **11 percent** of Guatemalans say they do not align with **any** religion.

ARTS AND ENTERTAINMENT

Guatemala's rich culture has been influenced by the beliefs and traditions of its different peoples. The ancient Maya had unique styles of architecture, arts, and music. The arrival of the Spanish brought new styles and approaches to the surroundings. Over time, traditions have merged with modern styles to bring even more diversity to the country's arts and culture scene.

The work of Carlos Mérida, one of Guatemala's best-known artists, is influenced by Mayan styles. Juan Sisay was part of a group of Mayan artists that created works showing local communities, landscapes, and people. Antonio Coche Mendoza paints scenes showing everyday Guatemalan life, ranging from its festivals to its markets.

Traditional music continues to be played at festivals and other celebrations. Much of this music has been influenced by Spanish culture. Instruments commonly played in Guatemalan music include the marimba, guitar, and maracas.

Guatemala's craftspeople still create textiles using an ancient technique called backstrap weaving. It involves having the warp, or yarns, attached to both the weaver and a post or other solid object.

The Dance of the Moors is performed at fiestas in many of Guatemala's Spanish colonial villages. When the Spanish first arrived in the country, they taught the dance to the locals as a way to introduce them to Spanish culture and religion.

The country has produced several well-known musical artists. Folk singer Ricardo Arjona has sold more than 20 million records worldwide. Gaby Moreno, who writes song lyrics in Spanish, English, French, and Portuguese, has won multiple Grammy awards. Hip hop artist Rebecca Lane uses her voice to speak out against violence and inequality. Singer-songwriter Sara Curruchich sings in both Spanish and the Mayan language of Kaqchikel.

Gaby Moreno performed at the 2024 Grammy Awards in Los Angeles, California, where she won the award for Best Latin Pop Album.

Guatemala's storytelling, folklore, and literature draw deeply from the Mayan culture. The *Popol Vuh*, an ancient Mayan text, tells the stories of how Mayan gods created humans and the world. Author Rigoberta Menchú, winner of the 1992 Nobel Peace Prize, is known for her book, *I, Rigoberta Menchú*. It describes the devastating treatment the Maya have endured in the country. Miguel Ángel Asturias won the Nobel Prize for Literature in 1967. He created works in a style of writing called **magical realism**.

Film and entertainment are growing industries in Guatemala. The film *Ixcanul*, directed by Jayro Bustamante, won several international awards. Guatemalan actress María Mercedes Coroy gained international attention for her role in the film. Oscar Isaac, born in Guatemala City, has appeared in many Hollywood films.

In the years since the publication of her book, Rigoberta Menchú has continued to fight for Indigenous rights and social justice.

SPORTS

With such a vast range of natural landscapes, many people enjoy outdoor sports and activities in Guatemala. Hiking to the tops of volcanoes, exploring caves, and mountain biking are common pastimes. Swimming, surfing, and fishing are popular off the coasts.

Soccer is the most popular sport in Guatemala. Both the men's and women's national teams play at the Estadio Nacional Doroteo Guamuch Flores, in Guatemala City. Carlos Ruiz got his start at this stadium before becoming internationally known. Nicknamed *El Pescado*, or "the fish," Ruiz played for the Guatemalan national team as well as for the Los Angeles Galaxy, F.C. Dallas, Toronto F.C., Philadelphia Union, and D.C. United teams.

Guatemalan children can often be seen playing *chamusca*, or street soccer.

In 2016, Carlos Ruiz became the highest scorer in World Cup qualifier history, with a total of 39 goals over the course of his career.

Basketball is also gaining attention in Guatemala. Ricardo Arjona was a professional basketball player before he made music his career. Ball sports played by the ancient Maya, such as pok-ta-pok, have recently seen increased interest. In pok-ta-pok, players move a rubber ball across a court using only their bodies. Points are scored by those who can get the ball through a large hoop that hangs above the court.

Pok-ta-pok has been played by Central America's Indigenous peoples since at least 1400 BC.

Many Guatemalan athletes have participated in global competitions, including the Olympic Games. Erick Barrondo won a silver medal in racewalking during the 2012 Olympics in London. He was the first person from Guatemala to win an Olympic medal. At the Paris Olympics in 2024, Adriana Ruano Oliva made history when she became the first Guatemalan Olympian to win a gold medal. She competed in the women's trap shooting event.

Adriana Ruano Oliva achieved her gold medal on only her second Olympic appearance. She had also participated in the 2020 Summer Games in Tokyo, Japan, where she finished 26th in the competition.

QUIZ TIME

Test your knowledge of Guatemala by answering these questions.

1 How many volcanoes does Guatemala have?

2 What is the name of Guatemala's best-known soccer player?

3 How many geographic regions does Guatemala have?

4 How many languages are spoken in Guatemala?

5 When did Guatemala declare its independence from Spain?

6 What is Guatemala's national bird?

7 How many branches of government are there in Guatemala?

8 Who was the first Guatemalan to win an Olympic gold medal?

9 What percentage of people living in Guatemala are Maya?

10 How much of Guatemala's total area does the Maya Biosphere Reserve cover?

ANSWERS
1. More than 30
2. Carlos Ruiz
3. Three
4. 25
5. 1821
6. The resplendent quetzal
7. Three
8. Adriana Ruano Oliva
9. 40 percent
10. 20 percent

KEY WORDS

active: currently erupting or likely to erupt
architecture: the art or science of building
artifacts: objects made by humans in the past
civil war: a war between opposing groups of citizens of the same country
cloud forests: humid tropical forests that have almost constant cloud cover
congress: the supreme legislative body of a nation, especially of a republic
conquistadors: leaders in the Spanish conquest of America
corruption: dishonest or illegal behavior, especially by powerful people
coup: the overthrow or alteration of an existing government by a small group
democratic republic: a form of government in which political power resides in the people
dictators: leaders who hold complete, unlimited governmental power
dormant: marked by a suspension of activity
ecosystems: a community of organisms and their physical environment interacting
encomienda: a system that granted Spanish adventurers and settlers the legal right to extract forced labor from Indigenous tribal chiefs
endangered: close to becoming extinct
endemic: native and restricted to a certain place
enslave: to force into slavery
exports: goods sold and shipped to another country
federation: a group of organizations, countries, or regions that have joined together to form a larger organization or government
gross domestic product (GDP): the total value of all the goods and services produced in a country's economy
imports: goods brought into a country for sale
magical realism: a literary genre or style associated especially with Latin America that incorporates fantastic or mythical elements into otherwise realistic fiction
Mayan civilization: an early American civilization that thrived from around 2000 BC to the Spanish conquest in the 16th century AD
nomadic: people who have no fixed residence but move from place to place, usually seasonally and within a well-defined territory
prey: an animal hunted for food
rural: of or relating to the countryside
spelunkers: people who make a hobby of exploring and studying caves
status quo: the existing state of affairs
tropical storm: a cyclone with strong winds of more than 39 miles (63 km) per hour but less than hurricane intensity

INDEX

animals 7, 12, 13, 18

Chichicastenango 16, 17
climate 10, 11, 12
cloud forests 12, 16

economy 14, 15, 23
El Petén 10, 16

government 4, 6, 9, 14, 20, 21, 22, 23, 30
Guatemala City 5, 9, 14, 17, 20, 23, 27, 28

Indigenous peoples 6, 20, 21, 24, 25, 27, 29

Lake Atitlán 9, 16, 23
language 5, 24, 25, 27, 30
literature 27

Maya 4, 7, 9, 16, 18, 20, 21, 24, 25, 26, 27, 29, 30
Maya Biosphere Reserve 12, 13, 16, 30
music 7, 9, 17, 24, 26, 27, 29

National Palace 6, 17

Pacific Ocean 8
plants 7, 12, 13
pyramids 4, 16

rainforests 6, 12, 13, 16
religion 19, 25, 26
rivers 9, 10, 16

Spain 5, 17, 18, 19, 21, 24, 25, 26, 27, 30
sports 28, 29

temples 4, 16
Tikal 16, 18

United States 15

Villa Nueva 23
volcanoes 6, 9, 10, 16, 28, 30

GUATEMALA 31

Get the best of both worlds.

AV2 bridges the gap between print and digital.

The expandable resources toolbar enables quick access to content including **videos**, **audio**, **activities**, **weblinks**, **slideshows**, **quizzes**, and **key words**.

Animated videos make static images come alive.

Resource icons on each page help readers to further **explore key concepts**.

Published by Lightbox Learning Inc.
276 5th Avenue, Suite 704 #917
New York, NY 10001
Website: www.openlightbox.com

Copyright ©2026 Lightbox Learning Inc.
All rights reserved. No part of this publication may be reproduced, stored in a retrieval system, or transmitted in any form or by any means, electronic, mechanical, photocopying, recording, or otherwise, without the prior written permission of the publisher.

Library of Congress Cataloging-in-Publication Data
Names: Banting, Erinn author.
Title: Guatemala / Erinn Banting.
Description: New York, NY : Lightbox Learning Inc, [2026] | Series: Central America | Includes index. | Audience: Grades 4-6
Identifiers: LCCN 2025003989 (print) | LCCN 2025003990 (ebook) | ISBN 9798874521226 lib. bdg. | ISBN 9798874521233 paperback | ISBN 9798874521240 ebook other | ISBN 9798874521257 ebook other
Subjects: LCSH: Guatemala--Juvenile literature | Guatemala--Description and travel--Juvenile literature
Classification: LCC F1463.2 .B36 2026 (print) | LCC F1463.2 (ebook) | DDC 972.81--dc23/eng/20250324
LC record available at https://lccn.loc.gov/2025003989
LC ebook record available at https://lccn.loc.gov/2025003990

Printed in Guangzhou, China
1 2 3 4 5 6 7 8 9 0 29 28 27 26 25

042025
101324

Project Coordinator Heather Kissock
Designer Terry Paulhus
Layout Mandy Christiansen

The publisher has made every reasonable effort to trace ownership and to obtain permission to use copyright material. The publisher would be pleased to have any errors or omissions brought to its attention so that they may be corrected in subsequent printings. Some visual elements in this title may have been generated using AI. While we strive for accuracy in all aspects of our products, we cannot guarantee that the elements depicted in these images are accurate. The publisher acknowledges Getty Images, Alamy, Bridgeman Images, and Wikimedica Commons as the primary image suppliers for this title. If you have any inquiries about these images or would like to provide any feedback, please reach out to us at feedback@openlightbox.com

All of the Internet URLs and Google Maps links given in the interactive eBook were valid at the time of publication. However, due to the dynamic nature of the Internet, some addresses may have changed, or sites may have ceased to exist since publication. While the author and publisher regret any inconvenience this may cause readers, no responsibility for any such changes can be accepted by either the author or the publisher.